GERMAN AIRSHIPS

PARSEVAL-SCHUTTE-LANZ-ZEPPELIN

HEINZ J. NOWARRA

1469 Morstein Road, West Chester, Pennsylvania 19380

BIBLIOGRAPHY:

Schmalenbach: Die deutschen Marine-Luftschiffe, 1928
Engberding: Luftschiff und Luftschiffahrt, 1932
Nowarra: 50 Jahre Deutsche Luftwaffe, Vol. 1-3, 1961
Busch/von Forstner: Krieg auf sieben Ozeanen; Chapter: Küster, Marine-Luftschiffe, 1935
Rasch/Hormel, Taschenbuch der Luftflotten, 1914
American Heritage: History of Flight, 1962
E. A. Lehmann: Auf Luftpatrouille und Weltfahrt, 1938
Schütte: Der Luftschiffbau Schütte-Lanz, 1926
Feldgrau: Die deutschen Heeres-und Marine-Luftschiffe, 1960
Lennat Ege: Ballons und Luftschiffe, 1973
Peter Meyer: Das grosse Luftschiffbuch, 1976

PHOTOS:

Nowarra Archives
Provan Archives

Originally published under the title "Deutsche Luftschiffe", copyright Podzun-Pallas-Verlag, 6360 Friedberg 3 (Dorheim), © 1988, ISBN: 3-7909-0332-9.

Translated from the German by Dr. Edward Force.

Copyright © 1990 by Schiffer Publishing.
Library of Congress Catalog Number: 89-063353.

Printed in the United States of America.
ISBN: 0-88740-199-6

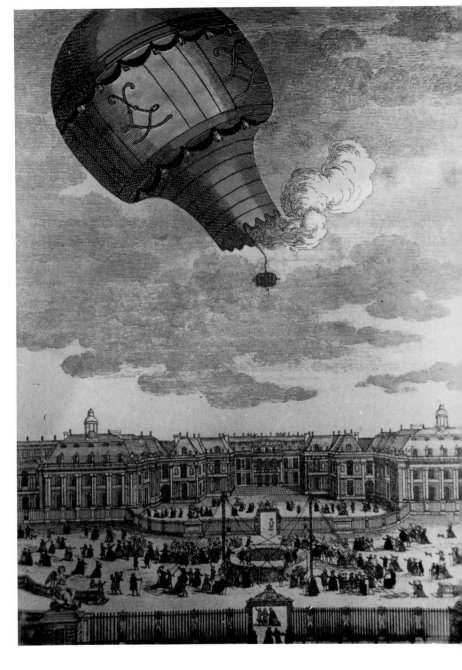

On September 19, 1783 the brothers Etienne and Joseph Montgolfier for the first time sent up a hot-air balloon, whose passengers were a sheep, a duck and a rooster, all of whom made the trip unharmed.

THE FORERUNNERS OF AIRSHIP TRAVEL

The idea of flying like the birds is as old as mankind. Tales and legends dealt with the theme even before Christ was born, as the legend of Daedalus and Icarus proves.

At first various inventors tried to fly with machines that were heavier than air. Only toward the end of the 18th Century did the Montgolfier brothers in France get the idea of rising into the air with the help of a hot-air balloon. On July 5, 1783 the first ascension of such a balloon took place, and thus "lighter-than-air aviation" was born.

The Montgolfier brothers were laymen, inspired only by their idea.

The scientist Professor Charles then used hydrogen to fill the balloon, so that the balloon material would not be in danger of burning, as was the case with the hot-air balloon. In September of 1783 he made his first flight with a companion in a hydrogen-filled balloon. The army quickly made use of this new invention. England first used balloons for military purposes in 1793. One year later France set up the first airship unit; Germany followed ten years later.

But the balloon was always dependent on the prevailing wind direction. Thus the desire arose to make the balloon steerable. In 1853 Henri Giffard built an airship with a 3-HP steam engine as its powerplant, with which a speed of two to three meters per second was achieved in calm air. Experiments by Hähnlein in Germany in 1872 and the Tissandier brothers in France in 1881 were similarly unsatisfactory. In 1885 Colonel Renard built the airship "La France" with an 8.5-HP electric motor and airscrew. With it a speed of 6.5 meters per second was attained. The form of this airship, already aero-dynamically good, was noteworthy. In

Professor Charles and Pilatre de Rozier succeeded in launching from the Tuileries, in September of 1783, the first manned balloon flight with the "Charlière", a balloon filled with hydrogen. The flight lasted four hours and covered a distance of 63 kilometers.

3

Germany ten years later, David Schwarz got the idea of building a fully rigid airship in the form of a bullet, its aluminum framework covered with a skin of sheet aluminum. A 12-HP Daimler motor provided the power. After a short test flight, though, this ship was lost in a forced landing on November 3, 1897. Later Schwarz spent years bringing lawsuits for alleged patent violation against Count Zeppelin, which ruined him financially without bringing any success. Lieutenant General z.D. Ferdinand, Count von Zeppelin had already been working since 1873 on the concept of a rigid airship in which gas cells built into a framework would lift the ship. As early as 1887 he presented a memorandum to King Karl of Württemberg, expressing his ideas in writing and thereby proving that he was the first, even before David Schwarz, to have had the idea for a rigid airship.

Three types of airship are differentiated: non-rigid, in which the gondola with the powerplant hangs from a net that is placed over the balloon. The permanence of the form is maintained by the so-called "Ballonett". The semi-rigid system, used for the Parseval, Gross-Basenach, Siemens-Schuckert, Veeh and others, is characterized by a keel construction firmly attached to the non-rigid balloon. Airships of this type are still built, chiefly in the USA (blimps). The rigid type was built by Zeppelin as well as at the Lanz factories in Rheinau and Zeesen, based on ideas of Professor Schütte. The aerodynamically more favorable form conceived by Professor Schütte, compared to the original "cigar shape" of the Zeppelin airships, was also adopted by the latter during World War I.

While almost exclusively semi-rigid airships were built and used for military purposes in France and England, in Germany the rigid type used by Zeppelin and Schütte-

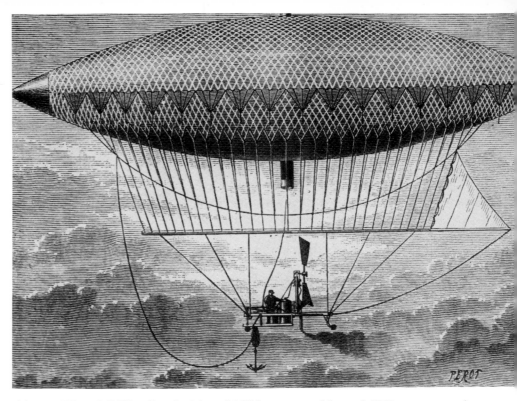

Above: Henri Giffard's airship of 1853, powered by a 3-HP steam engine.

Below: Hänlein's airship of 1872, driven by a gas engine.

Lanz prevailed more and more, the two differing mainly in that Zeppelin used an aluminum framework and Schütte-Lanz a wooden one. World War I drove their development into a mad rush.

Above: In 1895 David Schwarz built this all-metal airship with a 12-HP Daimler motor. It crashed on November 3, 1897.

Below: First launching of the Parsefal PL 1 airship in 1901.

In 1909 the Steffen Brothers built this semi-rigid airship in Kronshagen, near Kiel.

5

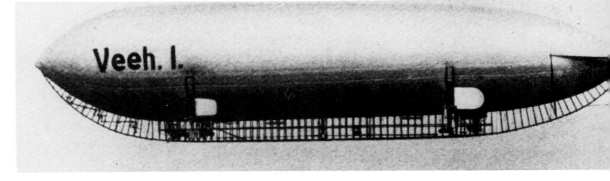

GERMAN AIRSHIP CONSTRUCTION UP TO AUGUST 1914

In the last years before the outbreak of World War I, various airships were developed, in part through private initiative. In the end, though, an airship-building industry developed, with which individual entrepreneurs could not compete because they lacked military support. Among others, there were the Clouth dirigible in Frankfurt am Main in 1908/1909, the Steffen brothers' airship in Kronshagen, near Kiel, the "Veeh" airship, the "Erslöh" dirigible, and the Siemens-Schickert airship, a giant in its day. Because of the army's and navy's interest, though, only the airships of Major von Parseval, and that of Major Gross and Engineer Basenach, could prevail. All of these craft belonged to the non-rigid or semi-rigid construction type. The Parseval craft were built by the Luftfahrzeug GmbH of Berlin in their Bitterfeld yard, while the Gross-Basenach airships were built in the airship yards of the Prussian military command in Berlin-Tegel. Yet none of these ships saw service on the front as of 1914. The situation was very different for the rigid airships built by the Schütte-Lanz firm of Rheinau, Baden, and the Zeppelin works in Friedrichshafen.

At the Luftfahrzeug GmbH (LFG), after the first experimental craft, the airships PL 1 to PL 14 were built between 1906 and the outbreak of the war. Of these, PL 4 was sold to Austria, PL 9 to Turkey, PL 13 to Japan, and PL 7 and PL 14 to Russia. Of the three craft built by Schütte-Lanz, SL 1 (1908/09) and SL 2 (1913/14) went to the Prussian military command and SL 3, as L 4, to the Imperial Navy.

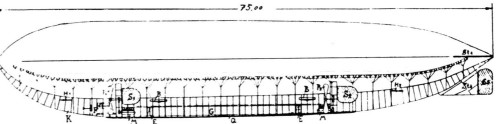

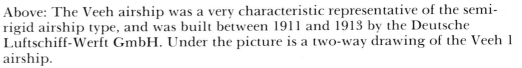

Above: The Veeh airship was a very characteristic representative of the semi-rigid airship type, and was built between 1911 and 1913 by the Deutsche Luftschiff-Werft GmbH. Under the picture is a two-way drawing of the Veeh 1 airship.

Below: In 1911/12 Siemens-Schuckert built the semi-rigid SS 1 airship from designs by Krell and Dietzius in Berlin-Biesdorf. Under the photo is a two-way drawing of the Siemens-Schuckert SS 1.

But the greatest airship builder, even though after numerous failures and disappointments, was the firm of "Luftschiffbau Zeppelin GmbH" founded by Count Zeppelin.

The experimental craft LZ 1, built in 1900, was disassembled the very next year after several flights. In 1905 the Zeppelin airship LZ 2 was finished, but on January 18, 1906 it crashed while landing at Kisslegg. On October 9, 1906, thanks to money provided by a lottery approved by the King of Württemberg, the LZ 3 made its maiden flight. The test flights gave excellent results. Even Zeppelin's competitor, Major Gross, had to admit that this airship met the demands of the time. During this testing, which led to the acceptance of LZ 3 by the German Empire, Count Zeppelin made the acquaintance of Dr. Hugo Eckener, who was to be his helper from then on and complete his life's work. LZ 3 was lengthened on 1909, and on November 10, 1908 it was taken over by the army as Z I, serving uneventfully until 1913 as a training ship for the young airship crews. The next craft built, LZ 4, was destroyed at Echterdingen on August 5, 1908. Zeppelin's work seemed to have come to an end at that point. But a miracle happened: The entire German people helped with contributions that totaled more than six million Reichsmarks. But the next ship, LZ 5, also had bad luck: After several successful flights, it was destroyed in a storm near Weilburg on April 25, 1910. Despite further misfortunes, LZ 7 through LZ 24 were built in quick succession until 1913. Of them, LZ 7 "Deutschland" was stranded in the Teutoburg Forest on January 28, 1910, LZ 8 "Ersatz-Deutschland" (Substitute Germany) was destroyed on May 16, 1911 while leaving its hangar at Düsseldorf. LZ 10 "Schwaben" burned in front of its Düsseldorf hangar on June 28, 1912. LZ 11 "Sachsen" went to the DELAG, a firm founded to carry on air transportation.

Above: In 1912 the Parseval airship PL 12 'Charlotte' was built; it is shown here at an intermediate stop in Wanne-Herten.

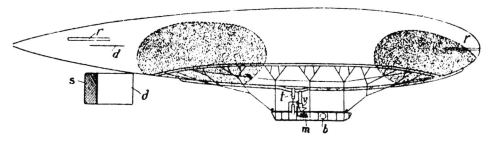

Cutaway drawing of the Parseval P III.

Below: In 1908 the airship M 1 was built in Berlin-Tegel, to the designs of Major Gross and Engineer Basenach.

Above: Gross-Basenach M 3 was built in 1910, then enlarged in 1911 from 7000 to 9000 cubic meter capacity, as can be seen clearly by the hull.

Below: M 4 too, built in 1911, was enlarged in 1913 from 9960 to 13,000 cubic meter capacity, but was not satisfactorily after it was rebuilt. Under the picture is a side-view drawing of the Gross-Basenach airship m 4.

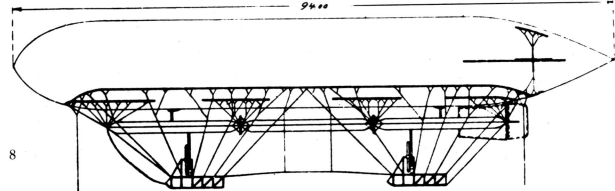

LZ 6 burned in its hangar in Baden-Oos on September 14, 1910. LZ 15 (Replacement Z I) was destroyed near Karlsruhe on March 19, 1913. LZ 14 went to the navy as L 1 and went down in a storm near Helgoland on September 9, 1913. LZ 9 went to the Prussian military command as Z II. So did LZ 12 as Z III and LZ 16 as Z IV. LZ 18 went to the navy as L 2 and burned before the eyes of hundreds of horrified spectators at Johannisthal, near Berlin, on October 17, 1913. LZ 19, as well as LZ 20 to LZ 24, all went to the Prussian military command.

The airships built by the Gross-Basenach system until 1913, M 1 to M 4, were all rebuilt one or more times but could not satisfy military requirements. M 3 burned in its hangar at Tegel on September 13, 1911.

How much importance was placed on the military value of airships can also be seen in the construction of airships landing fields and hangars. Airship facilities existed in:

Aachen, Cologne-Bickendorf, Berlin-Biesdorf, Bitterfeld, Braunschweig, Cuxhafen, Dresden, Düsseldorf, Frankfurt am Main, Friedrichshafen, Hamburg-Fuhlsbüttel, Gotha, Graudenz, Hannover, Berlin-Johannisthal, Kiel, Königsberg (East Prussia), Leichlingen, Leipzig, Liegnitz, Mantzell, Metz, Baden-Baden-Oos, Potsdam, Posen, Mannheim-Rheinau, Schneidemühl, Strassburg, Berlin-Tegel, Thorn (West Prussia), Trier and Wanne.

While the army conceived of the airship primarily for use in bombing attacks on enemy hinterlands, the Imperial Navy regarded the airship chiefly as a means of extensive long-range reconnaissance over the ocean, which could not be accomplished with the seaplanes of the time.

How important the Zeppelin airships were considered by their future opponents is shown by the fate of Z IV (LZ 16) on April 13, 1913: LZ 16 took off with the military acceptance

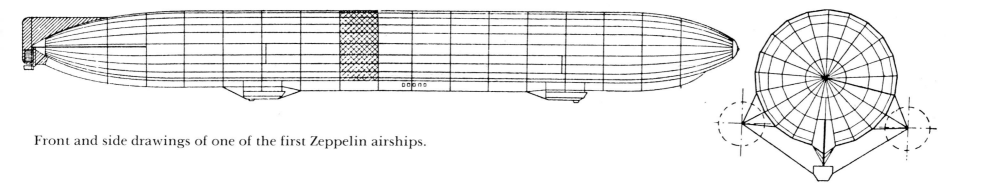

Front and side drawings of one of the first Zeppelin airships.

commission of Captain George, First Lieutenant Brandeis, First Lieutenant Felix Jacobi and its pilot, Captain Glund, and landed at the French airport of Lune/ville through a navigational error. The French used this lucky opportunity to study the German construction thoroughly. Then Z IV was freed to leave. After this information was gained, changes were made in the rigid airship of the French engineer Spiess, under construction since 1912, though it never saw service at the front. A photo of this airship shows its German "ancestry".

Right: Takeoff of the first Zeppelin airship, LZ 1, on July 2, 1900.

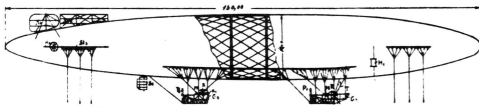

Above: The rigid airship SL 1 was built from designs by Professor Schütte at the Lanz yards in Rheinau between 1909 and 1911. Below is a side-view drawing of the Schütte-Lanz SL 1.

Below: Wreck of the airship LZ 2 after an accident in Kisslegg, in the Allgäu, on January 17, 1906.

Above: LZ 4 was built in 1908 and destroyed near Echterdingen on August 5 of the same year.

Below: The DELAG airship LZ 7 "Deutschland", here emerging from its hangar in Baden-Oos, was wrecked in the Teutoburger Wald on June 28, 1910.

LZ 5, army airship Z II, landing at Limburg on the Lahn, October 24, 1910.

LZ 5 at Limburg on October 24, 1910—one day before the storm.

The wreck of the Z II (LZ 5) after the storm in Weilburg on October 25, 1910.

Above: Count Zeppelin (left) and Dr. Eckener (right) in the pilot's gondola of LZ 10, "Schwaben", in 1910.

Below: Two-view drawing of LZ 10, "Schwaben".

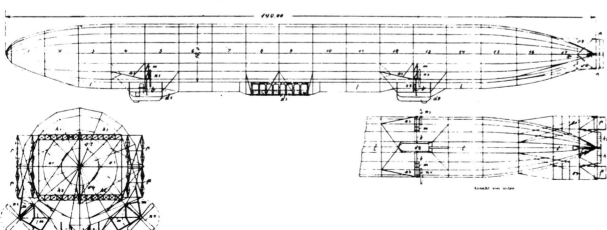

Above: Dr. Hugo Eckener, the man who saw his life's purpose in the struggle for the concept of the Zeppelin airship.

Below: Chief Constructor Dr. Dürr directed the technical work of the Zeppelin firm from LZ 1 to LZ 129.

LZ 6, built in 1909, going into the floating hangar on Lake Constance.

Landung des Zeppelin-Luftschiffes „Schwaben" in Johannisthal.

LZ 11, "Viktoria Luise", carried passengers for the DELAG organization.

LZ 10, "Schwaben", landing in Johannisthal, near Berlin.

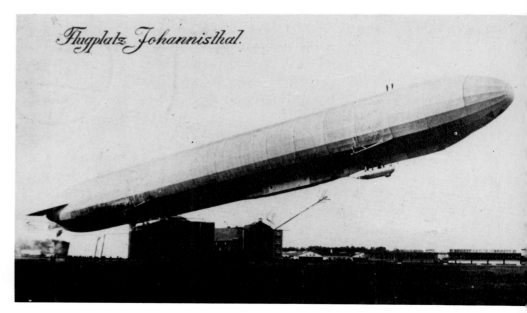

Flugplatz Johannisthal.

LZ 13, "Hansa", was another DELAG ship, seen here being launched at Johannisthal.

15

LZ 13, "Hansa", flies over a sailing regatta near Kiel in 1913.

Another picture of "Hansa" over Kiel Bay during Kiel Week in 1913.

Upper right: LZ 14, as the first airship of the Imperial Navy, was designated L 1. It was lost on September 9, 1913 in a storm near Helgoland.

Right: LZ 16 (Z IV) made a forced landing at Luneville, France, on April 3, 1913.

Above: LZ 17, "Sachsen", flew for DELAG, under Captain Lehmann, until war broke out, and then, with the same commander, was based in Cologne and did long-range reconnaissance in the west.

Below: After they had evaluated what they learned from the landing of Z IV in Luneville, the French launched their "Spiess" airship in new form in 1914.

Above: The rear gondola of army airship Z IV (LZ 16).

Below: Z VI (LZ 21) was lost in a crash-landing in the woods near Bonn on the way back from its first war mission against Liege.

THE GERMAN AIRSHIPS IN WORLD WAR I

When war broke out in August of 1914, the army possessed Zeppelin airships Z IV, Z V, Z VI, Z VII, Z VIII, Z IX and the airships "Viktoria Luise" and "Hansa", just taken out of passenger service. In addition, it had the Schütte-Lanz airship SL 2 and the Parseval P IV. The army airships were stationed as follows at the beginning of the war:

Z VI	Captain Kleinschmitt	Cologne
Z VII	Captain Jacobi	Baden-Oos
Z VIII	Captain André	Trier
Z IX	(Hansa) Captain Horn	Düsseldorf
Viktoria Luise	Captain Lempertz	Frankfurt am Main

These six ships were under the direct control of the Army High Command. Only Z IV, under Captain von Quast, was under the Eighth Army in Königsberg.

Right: the Schütte-Lanz airship SL 2 made its first flight on February 28, 1914 and was taken over by the Prussian military command.

Below: Two-way drawing of the Schütte-Lanz SL 2.

The Imperial Navy possessed one airship, namely L 3, commanded by Lieutenant Commander Fritz.

SL 2 and P IV served only for training. Z V had already been lost on August 28, 1914. It was obvious that the climbing ability of airships over land was insufficient, for on August 23 Z VII and Z VIII were both lost, as was Z IX on October 8, 1914. Thus after a month of air war the army had only Z IV, used for reconnaissance in the east, and the former passenger airship "Viktoria Luise", used only for training. Thus the sacrifice of airshipmen began, as can be seen just from the following figures: The army had 27 Zeppelin airships and four Schütte-Lanzcraft in service by the end of the war. Of them, only LZ 113, LZ 120 and SL 22 survived the war.

The constantly increasing losses of army airships led in 1917 to the end of military airship use. The successes achieved by them during bombing attacks could not justify the huge losses of men and material.

The situation developed very differently in the Imperial Navy. This was due in part to the fact that the naval airships operated mainly over water and needed to penetrate only comparatively slightly into British air space, while the army airships always had to operate over the front in the west. The second reason was based on the fact that the Imperial Navy had a "leader of airships" in the truest sense in Corvette Captain Peter Strasser, whose accomplishments simply cannot be valued highly enough.

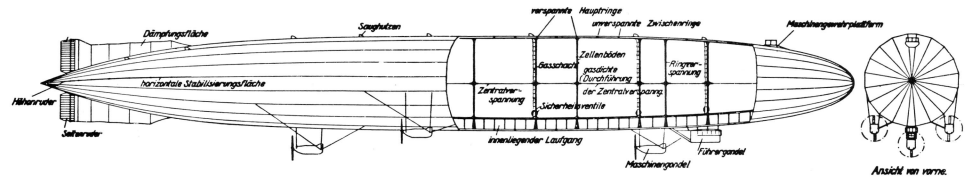

Schütte-Lanz 2.

L = 144 m, S = 18,2 m; V₁ = 24 500 m³, Größte Höhe 22,7 m, PS = 720, v = 24,5 m/s, Baujahr 1913. Probefahrt 28. Februar 1914.

The ruins of L 3 (LZ 24) after it crashed at Fano, Denmark on December 17, 1915.

Below: Army airship Z X (LZ 29) was lost at St. Quentin on March 20, 1915.

Even though the navy had but a single airship, they had provided early for the housing of additional ships. A turning double hangar stood ready at Nordholz. It remained the only one. During the war, for reasons of economy, only fixed hangars were built, a mistake that would revenge itself bitterly.

The Marine Airship Department (MLA), already in existence since 1912, was transferred from Fuhlsbüttel to Nordholz in October of 1914. The anticipated additional airships, along with L 3, were to serve in reconnaissance for the High Sea Fleet as well as securing fleet advances and mine-sweeping flotillas.

The Zeppelin yards in Friedrichshafen worked at top speed and were able to place six more airships, L 4 to L 9, at the disposal of the navy by March of 1915. They guarded the Bay of Helgoland and flew long-range reconnaissance in the whole area between the English east coast and the coast of Norway. They also watched over the approaches to the Baltic Sea, functioned as submarine chasers, and reported new English mine-laying activities.

In the night of January 19/20, 1915 the first attack of multiple airships on England took place. L 3 and L 4 attacked military targets on the English east coast with incendiary and explosive bombs. L 6 had to turn back because of heavy rainstorms near Terschelling. L 3 and L 4 were lost in a snowstorm about a month later. Fortunately, the human losses were not too high: only four men of L 4 were driven out to sea with the wreck and drowned. Meanwhile, additional ships came into service: Schütte-Lanz delivered SL 3 and SL 4, and the Luft-Fahrzeug-Gesellschaft provided PL 19 and PL 25.

The English very soon recognized the danger that threatened them from the airships. In the process, they had no regard for the neutrality of Holland and Switzerland. Flying over Holland, they destroyed **Z IX** in its hangar in Düsseldorf. From Switzerland they attacked Friedrichshafen, where **L 7**, still under construction, escaped being destroyed. Their attack on Nordholz was a mistake for the English. **L 5** had already spotted the launching of seaplanes from their mother ships in the Bay of Helgoland and drawn the correct conclusions. The attack broke up even before reaching its target.

L 9 belonged to an improved type, which had 600 kilometers more range than its forerunners because its volume had been increased by 2500 cubic meters. After a very brief training of its crew, the ship took part in a bombing attack on England on April 15, in which, thanks to its increased carrying ability, could carry almost 1000 kilograms of bombs. Along with L 9, L 5, L 6 and L 7 also took part in this squadron attack under unified command. The attack was led by Corvette Captain Strasser.

While still over the sea, L 7 was so badly shot up by English ships that it had to turn back. L 6 was also damaged but was able to carry out the attack.

The fact that the airships had a great tactical value was proved by the stopping of English advances into the Bay of Helgoland when the English naval forces saw that they had been spotted by airships. In good flying weather, the German fleet had a tactical superiority with the help of the airships, and the English knew well how important it was. In such weather conditions they avoided advances into the inner North Sea. On July 4, 1915 L 6, L 9 and L 10 discovered a group of aircraft mother ships and destroyer escorts north of Ameland and Terschelling at about 4:30 A.M. When L 10 appeared, the group

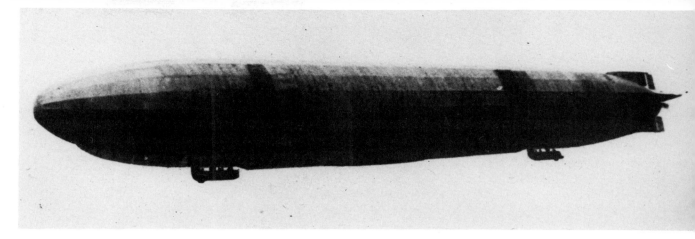

Above: LZ 37 was also an army airship, which was shot down over Ghent on June 7, 1915. It was hit by Lt. Warneford of the Royal Flying Corps.

Below: Army airship LZ 86, factory number LZ 56, saw service mainly on the eastern front.

Above: Naval airship L 10 (LZ 40) went into service on May 13, 1915, but was destroyed by a bolt of lightning near Cuxhaven on September 3, 1915.

Above: This picture of naval airship L 12 (LZ 43) shows clearly the addition of a machine-gun position atop the front of the ship.

Below: L 13 (LZ 45) flew from July 23, 1915 to April 25, 1917, and was then retired as obsolete at Hage, Holstein.

Below: L 12 (LZ 43) was badly damaged before Ostende on August 10, 1915 and its wreckage towed away by two torpedo boats.

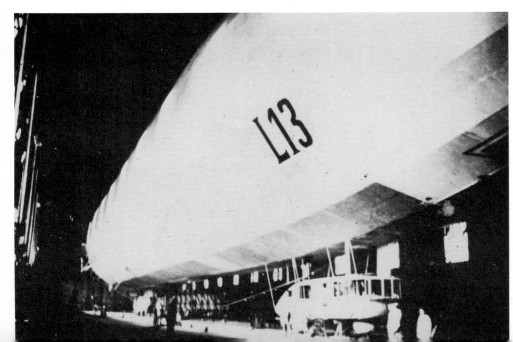

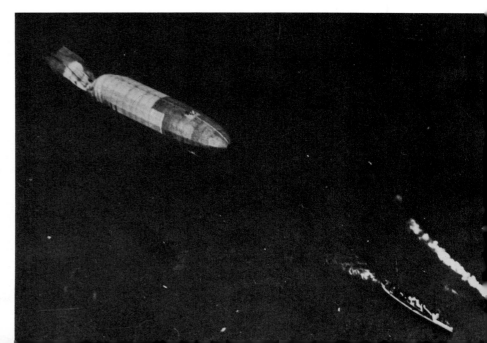

turned back to the west, where it was sighted by L 6, while L 9 was somewhat farther north. The English group headed for home at once.

The first attack on London had been attempted by Captain Beelitz with L 8 on February 26, 1915. Strong head winds forced him to turn back. On March 4 he tried again, but got into a bad storm, was hit by enemy flak, and had to land near Tirlemont, Belgium, where the airship was destroyed and the crew taken prisoner. Only on June 4, 1916 was Lieutenant Commander Hirsch able to reach London with L 10, dropping 30 explosive and 20 incendiary bombs.

On June 6, 1915 the first army airship was destroyed in an aerial battle during an attack of army and navy airships. It was already 1:00 A.M. on June 7 when the English Lieutenant Warneford spotted LZ 37 over Ostende. His Morane monoplane was considerably faster than the airship, which could only reach 96 kph. He caught up with it at Ghent, flew over it and dropped a bomb on the ship, which burst into flame at once. In the night of August 17/18, 1915, L 9, L 10, L 11, L 13 and L 14 attacked Hartlepool, Harwich and London, but only L 10, under First Lieutenant z. Wenke, reached London.

The losses in the first months of the war had shown that the performance of the airships had to be improved. It was mainly a question of their ability to ascend and carry loads. So new ships were built by Zeppelin, 163.5 meters long, with a volume of 31,900 cubic meters, a range of over 4000 kilometers and a ceiling of 3200 meters. At Schütte-Lanz they built SL 5, with a volume of 32,400 cubic

Above: A naval airship over the German High Sea Fleet. In the Battle of Jutland the weather prevented reconnaissance by airships.

Right: L 20 (LZ 59) crashed near Stavanger, Norway on May 3, 1916.

Naval airship LZ 72 (L 31) over the North Sea. It was lost over London on October 2, 1916.

Above: The semi-rigid airship Parseval PL 24 was put into service in 1914 but used only for training purposes.

Below: The Schütte-Lanz airship SL 7 was put into service in 1916 but retired as obsolete at the end of 1917.

meters, and SL 6 and SL 7, with 35,000 cubic meters. On September 8, 1915, L 11, L 13 and L 14, all ships of the 31,900 cubic meter type, took off to attack London. In the process, Lieutenant Commander Mathy, regarded by the English as the most successful airship captain, stood out in particular. Further attacks by army and naval airships troubled the English so much that Admiral Sir Percy Scott of the Royal Navy was put in charge of aerial defense. How much influence the German airships had on English personnel is shown by the fact that, according to English statistics, defence of their homeland required half a million men.

German airship attacks were intensified steadily, to be sure, but they were very dependent on the weather. Meanwhile a new, larger type was developed, with a capacity of 35,800 cubic meters; it could climb to 3500 meters and had a range of 4900 kilometers. The first two ships of this type took part in the big squadron attack on England on January 31, 1916. They were L 20 and L 21. Of the nine ships in action, L 14, L 19 and L 21 penetrated to the English west coast and bombed Liverpool and Birkenhead, L 13 and L 11 reached Hanley, and L15 and L 20 advanced to the coal-mining region around Sheffield. In this attack a tragedy occurred with L 19. The ship, commanded by Lieutenant Commander Loewe, came over The Netherlands, pushed by unfavorable weather, and was fired on. It was driven off and had to land at sea about a hundred nautical miles from Grimsby. Fifteen men survived, including Lieutenant Commander Loewe, who sent off a message in a bottle before he left the hulk that was floating in the water. In this situation the English fishing boat "King Stephen" found them and, despite calls for help, refused any assistance and watched as the German airshipmen drowned.

Above: Naval airship L 33 (LZ 76) was put in service on August 30, 1916, but was damaged during a bombing attack over London on September 24, 1916 and had to make a forced landing.

Above: Army airship LZ 77 (LZ 47) was lost over France on February 2, 1916.

Below: Naval airship L 34 (LZ 78, right), put in service on September 22, 1916, was lost in an attack over England on November 27, 1916.

Below: The pilot gondola of naval airship L 35 (LZ 80) before takeoff at Nordholz.

On March 25, 1916 the English tried to attack the airship hangars in Tondern with airplanes. The undertaking was a failure. Only two of the planes returned, and the attack never took place. Between the end of March and the end of May 1916, ten bomb attacks on English targets were made by the airships, with a maximum of seven ships taking part. In this attack, L 13 (Mathy), L 14 (Böcker) and L 16 stood out particularly. L 15, under Lieutenant Commander Breithaupt, was lost in an attack on North London. Breithaupt and his crew were taken prisoner. The army and navy airships now took turns making attacks, so that the English got the idea that the Germans were planning an invasion. On May 3, 1916 another hitherto successful ship, L 20, under Lieutenant Commander Stabbert, was lost. The head wind was so strong on the return trip that the ship could not reach Germany but had to land in Norway. The crew blew up the ship and was interned.

From July 28 to August 4, 1916 there were four successful attacks on England, in which up to ten airships took part. On September 2, two naval and four army airships flew over England and dropped bombs on military targets, doing considerable damage. In this attack, SL 11 was set afire by one of the English airship chasers. SL 11, which had a wooden frame, crashed near a small village named Cuffley and burned for two hours. Despite this loss, eleven naval airships attacked on September 11. This time a hitherto successful commander, First Lieutenant Peterson, now the commander of the big new airship L 32, met his fate. His ship was also ignited by gunfire. L 32 was the second ship of a new type with a capacity of 55,200 cubic meters, a range of 7400 km and a ceiling of 4000 meters. Its sister ship, L 33, under Lieutenant Commander Böcker, also had bad luck. His ship had dropped a well-

26

Above: Army airship LZ 81 (LZ 51) was put in service on the eastern front and crashed in Bulgaria on September 27, 1916. It is seen here before the hangar in Jamboli.

Below: Army airship LZ 85 (LZ 55) was shot down over southern France in 1916.

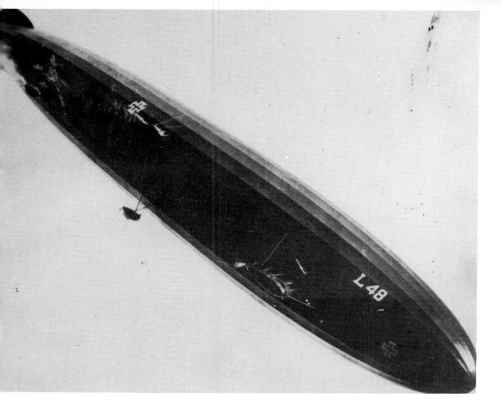

Above: L 48 (LZ 95) suffered the same fate as L 43 near Yarmouth on June 17, 1917.

Upper right: LZ 86 (LZ 56) at Wainoden in Courland during the winter of 1916.

Right: L 43 (LZ 92), put in service on March 6, 1917, was shot down by British airplanes over the North Sea on June 14, 1917.

aimed series of bombs on London despite heavy fire. On the way home, it was discovered that the ship was losing gas. It lost altitude and could not possibly have reached the Continent. So he decided to land in the vicinity of Colchester. He succeeded, but was not able to set fire to the ship, which had been put in service only on August 30. Thus on September 24, 1916 the almost undamaged ship fell into English hands. The components served as models for the **R 33** and **R 34** ships built in England in 1918/19.

In February of 1916, England's air defenses had been put in the hands of the British army, which set up ten airship defense units. This sealed the fate of the airships. The English soon came to view airship hunting as a sport. Despite this, the airship was still at the height of its success in the summer of 1916; only in 1917 did its downfall occur. In that year the army turned its airships over to the navy.

The year of 1917 brought the use of airships slowly to a stop. A certain advantage for night attacks was achieved by painting two-thirds of the lower part of the hull black. But the number of attacks on England decreased. In February of 1917, unlimited submarine warfare against England was declared. The airships were now used successfully in growing numbers to secure the arrivals and departures of the U-boats.

In 1917 there were only six airship attacks on England. It was found that the English had developed numerous ways of attacking the airships even before they reached Great Britain. In mid-May of 1917, **L 22** was shot down by a Felixstowe flying boat, a copy of the American Curtiss flying boat, while guarding light sea forces. On August 21, 1917, **L 23** was shot down by an airplane that took off from a small flight deck on board the British cruiser "Yarmouth". In March of

The commander of the airships, Corvette Captain Peter Strasser, and most of his airship commanders:

From left to right: Capt. Manger, L 41/L 62; Lt. Cmdr. Freudenreich, L 47/L 63; Lt. Cmdr. Schwonder, L 50; Capt. Prölss, L 37/L 53; Lt. Cmdr. Bockholt, L 23/L 44; Corv. Capt. Strasser; Lt. Cmdr. Geyer, L 16/L 49; Lt. Cmdr. Stabbert, L 20/L 44; Lt. Cmdr. Ehrlich, L 17/L 35/L 63; Lt. Cmdr. Martin Dietrich, L 9/L 22/L 38/L 42/L 71; Lt. Cmdr. Hollender, L 22/L 46; Lt. Cmdr. Dose, L 14/L 51/L 65; Lt. Cmdr. Friemel, L 30/L 52.

June 23, 1919: along with several others, as here in Nordholz, the crews of L 42 and L 63 destroyed their ships.

Below: Lieutenant Commander von Schiller and the last men of the naval airship unit in 1919.

Lieutenant Commander Martin Dietrich commanded L 9, L 22, L 38, L 42, then led one of the last attacks against England with L 71 (LZ 113).

33

L 70 (LZ 112) made a bombing attack on London under Corvette Captain Strasser on August 5, 1918, and fell victim to English fighter planes.

L 61 (LZ 106) survived the war but had to be turned over to Italy on August 28, 1920.

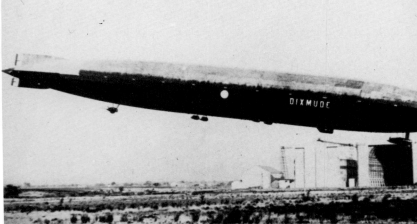

Above: L 72 (LZ 114), still under construction at war's end, had to be delivered to France on December 22, 1923; there it flew under the name "Dixmude".

Left: L 71 (LZ 113) was delivered to England on July 1, 1920, after having flown the last attack against England.

AIRSHIP CONSTRUCTION INSIDE AND OUTSIDE GERMANY AFTER 1919

As early as 1914 the British navy was using airships of the semi-rigid type for reconnaissance over the British sea zone. On the basis of the Zeppelin airships' success, contracts were given in 1914 for the first airships of the **R** (for rigid) class. The Vickers firm needed two years to produce the first of these craft, **R 23**. After the first Zeppelin airships were shot down over England and their wrecks had been examined intensively, an improved version was built, which was unsatisfactory because of its excessively heavy motors. Copies of the German **LZ 76 (L 33)**, designated **R 33** and **R 34**, were finished only in 1919. **R 34** then became the first airship to cross the Atlantic in both directions. The next ship, **R 36**, was intended for passenger traffic but went through several storms and was taken out of service in 1925. The following ship, **R 38**, crashed on August 24, 1921; only four men survived. The last R-ship was **R 80** (1921-1925), which spent only 73 hours in the air and was then dismantled.

Between 1919 and 1921 the small DELAG ships **LZ 120** "Bodensee" and **LZ 121** "Nordstern" were built in Germany. **LZ 120** had to be turned over to Italy and was used there under the name "Hesperia" until 1925. **LZ 121** became a reparations payment to France, where it was in service until 1927 under the name "Méditerranée". **LZ 124** and **LZ 125** remained projects. **LZ 126** went to the USA, also as reparations. It took off on October 12, 1924 for a flight across the Atlantic, landing on October 15 and being taken over by the U.S. Navy as **ZR 3** "Los Angeles". In 1936 it was taken out of service, but not dismantled until 1940. Right after its crossing, its filling of hydrogen was replaced by helium transferred from the **ZR 1** "Shenandoah", which was already in the

Above: The passenger airship "Bodensee" (LZ 120) had to be delivered to Italy after having made 103 trips between Friedrichshafen, Berlin and Stockholm and carrying 4050 passengers.

Below: LZ 121, "Nordstern" made its first flight on June 8, 1921, and had to be delivered to France on June 13.

USA. "Shenandoah" was the old German LZ 96 (L 49), that had landed undamaged in France in October of 1917. The USA wanted to build additional airships to this pattern.

"Shenandoah" took off for the first time with its helium filling on September 24, 1923, and made 57 flights despite a few critical situations, until it broke in three pieces in a storm on September 3, 1925 and its 29-man crew was lost.

The Italian semi-rigid airships "Norge" and "Italia" made headlines when Amundsen and General Nobile tried in vain to reach the North Pole with them.

Only the personal intervention of Dr. Eckener, Dr. Dürr and their colleagues managed to raise 2.5 million Marks, through contract trips in 1926/27, to pay for a new Zeppelin airship, LZ 127. The German government contributed 1.5 million. On July 8, 1928 the daughter of Count Zeppelin, Countess Brandenstein-Zeppelin, was able to christen LZ 127 with the name "Graf Zeppelin". It was a lucky ship, which was taken out of service only nine years later, after maintaining a regular mail and passenger service to Rio de Janeiro. It was set up as a museum, and destroyed only in 1940 on Göring's orders.

The LZ 128 project was dropped in favor of the improved design of LZ 129, the "Hindenburg". It was the most beautiful and modern airship that had ever been built. It was to come to grief through the fact that the USA would not release any helium to fill it. Once again the dangerous hydrogen had to be used.

In March of 1936, LZ 129 made a tour of Germany along with LZ 127. It was an unforgettable sight when the two giants of the air cruised low over Berlin and other cities. On May 4, 1937 LZ 129 set out on its first North Atlantic flight. In 1936 it had made 56 flights and carried 2656 passengers.

36

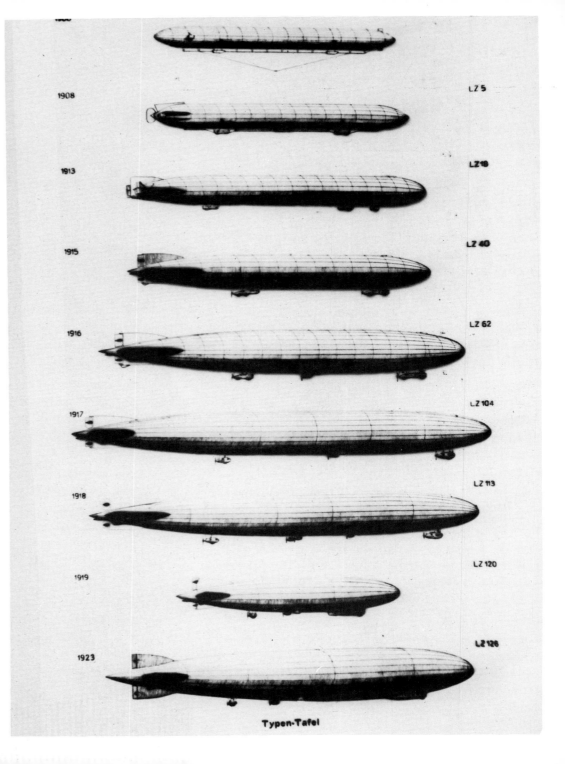

1908   LZ 5

1913   LZ 18

1915   LZ 40

1916   LZ 62

1917   LZ 104

1918   LZ 113

1919   LZ 120

1923   LZ 126

Typen-Tafel

On May 6, 1937 the "Hindenburg" came in to land at Lakehurst again. Shortly after 6:00 P.M. there was an explosion that turned the ship to a flaming hell as the hydrogen gas burst into glaring flames. Captain Pruss and Ernst Lehmann were the last to jump from the burning ship. Lehmann, one of the most experienced and successful airship pilots in war and peace, died the next day. Two thirds of the participants in the flight were dead or injured. The facts of the explosion have not been ascertained satisfactorily to this day.

Despite this fatal blow, Dr. Eckener did not give up, and LZ 130 was built. Eckener could even persuade the USA to release helium for the new ship. Then in 1938 German troops marched into Austria. The Americans immediately banned any export of helium. "For Eckener, yes, for Hitler not a single cubic centimeter." So the death sentence was passed on German airship travel.

In England the big airships R 100 and R 101 were built in 1929. R 100 did not seem to do its job and was dismantled in 1931. R 101 was lengthened after its first flight on October 14, 1929. On October 5, 1931, about 2:00 in the morning, R 101 exploded on its first planned flight to India. Forty-eight people died; only six survived.

As a reparations payment to the USA, ZR III (LZ 126) was finished in the summer of 1924. It is seen at right on its flight to the USA.

The airship Z R 3 leaves the hangar for the first time.

Das Luftschiff Z. R. 3 verläßt zum ersten Mal die Halle.

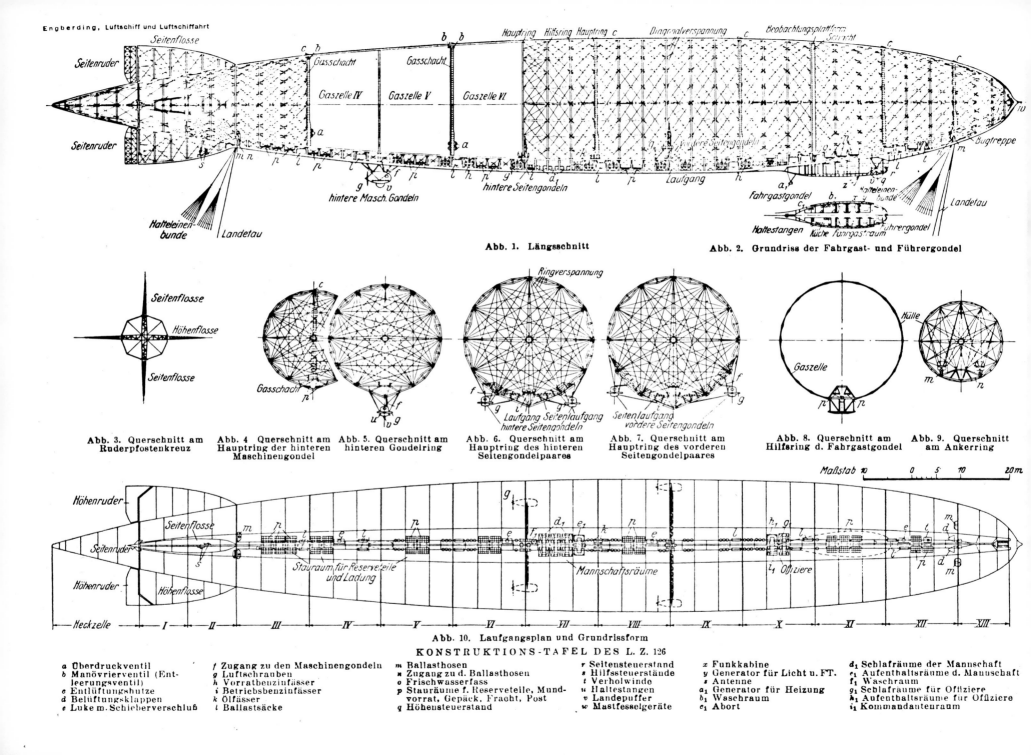

Engberding, Luftschiff und Luftschiffahrt

Abb. 1. Längsschnitt

Abb. 2. Grundriss der Fahrgast- und Führergondel

Abb. 3. Querschnitt am Ruderpfostenkreuz

Abb. 4 Querschnitt am Hauptring der hinteren Maschinengondel

Abb. 5. Querschnitt am hinteren Gondelring

Abb. 6. Querschnitt am Hauptring des hinteren Seitengondelpaares

Abb. 7. Querschnitt am Hauptring des vorderen Seitengondelpaares

Abb. 8. Querschnitt am Hilfsring d. Fahrgastgondel

Abb. 9. Querschnitt am Ankerring

Abb. 10. Laufgangsplan und Grundrissform

KONSTRUKTIONS-TAFEL DES L. Z. 126

a Überdruckventil	*f* Zugang zu den Maschinengondeln	*m* Ballasthosen	*r* Seitensteuerstand	*d₁* Schlafräume der Mannschaft
b Manövrierventil (Entleerungsventil)	*g* Luftschrauben	*n* Zugang zu d. Ballasthosen	*s* Hilfssteuerstände	*e₁* Aufenthaltsräume d. Mannschaft
c Entlüftungsshutze	*h* Vorratbenzinfässer	*o* Frischwasserfass	*t* Verholwinde	*f₁* Waschraum
d Belüftungsklappen	*i* Betriebsbenzinfässer	*p* Stauräume f. Reserveteile, Mundvorrat, Gepäck, Fracht, Post	*u* Haltestangen	*g₁* Schlafräume für Offiziere
e Luke m. Schieberverschluß	*k* Ölfässer	*q* Höhensteuerstand	*v* Landepuffer	*h₁* Aufenthaltsräume für Offiziere
	l Ballastsäcke		*w* Mastfesselgeräte	*i₁* Kommandanturaum
			x Funkkabine	
			y Generator für Licht u. FT.	
			z Antenne	
			a₁ Generator für Heizung	
			b₁ Waschraum	
			c₁ Abort	

After delivery to the USA, ZR III became a navy airship with the name "Los Angeles".

Above: "Los Angeles" was also anchored on the anchor mast of the "Patoka" at times.

Right: ZR III (LZ 126). called "Los Angeles" in the USA, flies over the Statue of Liberty in New York.

The English airship R 24 could not conceal its descent from the German Zeppelin airships.

On October 14, 1929 the English airship R 101 exploded on its first trip to India.

In the USA the Goodyear firm developed its small airships, of which the first, "Pony Blimp", was finished in 1919. The subsequent ships of this type had different names, but they were known in general as "Blimps". They were used mainly for advertising purposes and pleasure flights. Out of them, the U.S. Navy developed the K-Type for patrol flights and coast guarding. The "Blimps" are still flying today.

(Translator's note: I have read that the term "blimp" originated from the classification of these nonrigid airships as Class "B Limp" craft.)

Right:
The new "Graf Zeppelin" ship (LZ 127)

LZ 127 "Graf Zeppelin" over Lake Constance with the Do X flying boat in 1930.

LZ 129 ''Hindenburg'' (below) and LZ 127 ''Graf Zeppelin'' during their German cruise in 1936, year of the Olympic Games.

LZ 129 "Hindenburg" was put in service in 1935 as the second passenger airship of the German Zeppelin shipping organization.

Front motor gondola of LZ 129 "Hindenburg".

LZ 129 "Hindenburg" over the airship hangars in Friedrichshafen.

LZ 129 "Hindenburg" at Rhein-Main Airport, Frankfurt.

The terrible end of the "Hindenburg" on May 6, 1937 in Lakehurst, N.J., near New York.

The last German passenger airship, LZ 130—again bearing the name "Graf Zeppelin (II)"—was put in service in 1938, but because of the Lakehurst explosion it and LZ 127 were soon grounded.

Below: ZRS-5 "Macon" was lost with 83 men on February 11, 1935 in a rainstorm along the south coast of California. Its sister ship ZRS-4 "Akron" had already been lost over the Atlantic on October 27, 1931.

On the basis of plans drawn by the former airship expert Dr. Karl Arnstein, and based too on Zeppelin patents, ZRS-4 "Akron" was built in the USA in 1929-31. On October 27, 1931 the ship was lost in a storm over the Atlantic. Only three men survived. Its sister ship, ZRS-5 "Macon", had left its testing phase behind when it was caught in a rainstorm on February 11, 1935 and the entire tail, including the control surfaces, slowly divided into its component parts. Only two members of the 83-man crew survived; the rest died in the sea off the south coast of California.

After the catastrophes with R 100 and R 101 in England, "Akron" and "Macon" in the USA and the German LZ 129, the rigid airship was dead. Only the small nonrigid airships, such as Goodyear keeps on improving in the USA, has been able to survive to the present. In Germany, Engineer Naatz built three such airships using Parseval patents but could not compete with the financial might of the Goodyear firm. In 1971, Theo Wüllenkemper of Mülheim on the Ruhr tried to build similar ships. Despite initial success, he was not able to develop large models. Despite all this, the concept of airship transportation is not dead. In the USSR, work was being done in the Seventies on airship projects to open up Siberia. Somewhat later there appeared reports on the possibility of using airships to transport petroleum out of Arctic regions where the low temperatures made the use of pipelines impossible. In the USA there are still ideas of introducing rigid airships again, along the lines of the last German developments. Various organizations in Germany are trying to reawaken interest in airship travel.

In 1969 Dipl.Ing. Gerhard Hoffmann was called upon to build a new "Olympia Zeppelin", D-OZ 132, which was to be finished in four to five years. This was perhaps the last attempt to turn the idea of a German Zeppelin airship to reality.

All these attempts came to grief, though. Two reasons for this are clear: Because of the small supply of helium, available only in the USA, the cost of filling an airship of that type with helium is enormous. Enormous too are the costs of construction, as they would have to be based on fully new standpoints, and none of the old airship pilots or crewmen would be capable of serving in them. But one can still hope that the idealists who still dream of new airship travel today will one day find people with money and the willingness to risk a new beginning of airship flight.

Above and right:
Goodyear blimps as advertising craft in the Federal Republic of Germany.

PARSEVAL AIRSHIPS   Luftfahrzeug GmbH

1	2	3 cbm	4 m	5 h	6 PS	7 km/h	8 kg	9 m	10 vom	11 bis	12
P I	PL 2	4.000	60						09		H
P II	3	6.600	70						09	16. 5.11	H
PL 6	6	8.000	75	20	2 x 110	59	3.000	2.000	3. 6.10		M
P II Ers.	8	"	77	"	2 x 180	51	2.200	"	12. 2.10		H
P III	11	10.000	84	"	2 x 220	65	2.800	"	13.12.11		H
P IV	16	"	"	15	2 x 180	71	3.500	2.500	10.13		H.
PL 19	19	10.300	92		"	77	3.300	"	14	25. 1.15	M
+)	20										
+)	21										
+)	22										
+)	23										
+)	24										
PL 25	25	14.100	113,8		2 x 210	70	6.000	3.000	14		M
	26	31.150	157		4 x 240	90	18.600	4.500			
27	27	"	"		"	"	"	"			

MILITARY (GROSS) AIRSHIPS   Airship Yards of the Prussian Army Command

1	2	3 cbm	4 m	5 h	6 PS	7 km/h	8 kg	9 m	10 vom	11 bis	12
M a		1.400	41						07		H
M I		5.000	71						08		H
	U 09	5.200	71								H
	U 12	6.000	74		2 75	45	1.250				H
M II		5.200	71						09		H
	U 12	6.000									H
M III		7.000	83						10		H
	U 11	9.000	90								H
M IV		9.960	96						11		H
	U 13	13.000	97		3 x 150	75					H
	U 14	16.500				81	7.000				M

ERLÄUTERUNGEN SIEHE FOLGENDE SEITE!

1	2	3 cbm	4 m	5 h	6 PS	7 km/h	8 kg	9 m	10 vom	11 bis	12

SCHÜTTE-LANZ AIRSHIPS Luftschiffbau Schütte-Lanz

1	2	3 cbm	4 m	5 h	6 PS	7 km/h	8 kg	9 m	10 vom	11 bis	12
SL I	SL 1	19.500	131,-		2 x 240 /270	71	4.500	1.600	17.10.11	17. 7.13	H
II	2	23.000	144,-	24	4 x 180	80	8.000	2.500			H
3	3	32.400	165,-		4 x 210	86	13.400	2.700			M
4	4	”	”		”	”	”	”			M
5	5								7.15	3. 7.15	H
6	6	35.000	162,9		”	94	16.000	3.500			M
7	7	”	”		”	”	”	”	10.15		H
8	8	38.700	174,-		4 x 240	92	20.000	3.700	16		M
9	9	”	”		”	”	”	”	16		M
10	10	”	”		”	”	”	”	16	27. 7.16	H
11	11	”	”		”	”	”	”	8.16	2. 9.16	H
12	12	”	”		”	”	”	”			M
13	13	”	”		”	”	”	”			
14	14	”	”		”	”	”	”			M
15	15	”	”		”	”	”	”	12.16		H
+)	16										
+)	17										
+)	18										
+)	19										
20	20	56.000	198,3		5 x 240	104	35.500	4.500	17	5. 1.18	M
+)	21	”	”		”	”	”	”	5. 6.18	6.20	M
22	22	”	”		”	”	”	”			
+)	23										

Code for the tables of Parseval, Gross and Schütte-Lanz airships

1. Military designation
2. Manufacturer's designation
3. Volume of the airship: cubic meters
4. Length: meters
5. Range: hours
6. Engine power: HP
7. Top speed: kph
8. Weight: kilograms
9. Ceiling: meters
10. In service: from
11. Out of service or destroyed: to
12. H ' Army, M ' Navy

1	2	3	4	5	6	7	8	9	10	11	12
		cbm	m	km	PS	km/h	kg	m	vom	bis	

ZEPPELIN AIRSHIPS Luftschiffbau Zeppelin GmbH

1	2	3	4	5	6	7	8	9	10	11	12
Z I	Z 3	11.300	128,-		2 x 85				9.10.06		H
	U	12.200	136,-		2 x 115					13	H
Z II	LZ 5	15.000	"		2 x 105					25. 4.10	H
	9	16.550	132,-		3 x 145				2.10.11	1. 8.14	H
	U	17.800	140,-	1.600							
Viktoria Luise											
	LZ 11	18.700	148,-	1.100	3 x 170	76			14. 2.12	15	
Z III	12	17.800	140,-	1.600	3 x 145				25. 4.	14	H
Hansa	13	18.700	148,-	1.100	3 x 170	80			30. 7.	16	
L 1	14	22.465	158,-	2.800	3 x 165	76			7.10.	9. 9.13	M
Z I	15	19.550	142,-	2.700	3 x 170	"			16. 1.13	19. 3.13	H
Z IV	16	"	"	"	"	"			14. 3.	16	
Sachsen	17	"	141,-			"		2.000	30. 7.12		H
L 2	18	27.000	158,-	2.100	4 x 180	80			9. 9.13	17.10.13	M
Z I	19	19,550	140,-	2.700	3 x 180	77			6. 6.13	13. 6.14	H
Z V	20	"	"	"					8. 7.	28. 8.14	H
Z VI	21	20.870	148,-	1.900	"				10.11.	6. 8.14	H
Z VII	22	22.140	156,-	2.000	"				8. 1.14	23. 8.14	H
Z VIII	23	"	"	"	"				21. 2.	23. 8.14	H
L 3	24	22.470	158,-	2.200	3 x 210				11. 5.	17. 2.15	M
Z IX	25	"	"	"	"				29. 7.	8.10.14	M
Z XII	26	25.000	161,-	3.300	"	85	11.000	3.000	14.12.	8. 8.17	H
L 4	27	22.470	158,-	2.200	"	84	9.200	2.500	28. 8.	17.12.15	M
L 5	28	"	"	"	"	"	"	"	22. 9.	6. 8.15	M
Z X	29	"	"	"	"	"	"	"	13.10.	20. 3.15	H
Z XI	30	"	"	"	"	"	"	"	11.11.	20. 5.15	H
L 6	31	"	"	"	"	"	"	"	3.11.	19. 9.16	M
L 7	32	"	"	".	"	"	"	"	20.11.	4. 5.16	M
L 8	33	"	"	".	"	"	"	"	17.12.	5. 3.15	M
LZ 34	34	"	"	"	"	"	"	"	6. 1.15	21. 5.15	H
LZ 35	35	"	"	"	"	"	"	"	11. 1.	13. 4.15	H
L 9	36	24.900	161.4	2.800	"	85	11.000	3.000	8. 3.	16. 9.16	M
LZ 37	37	22.470	158,-	2.200	"	84	9.200	2.500	28. 2.	7. 6.15	H
LZ 38	38	31.900	163,5	4.300	"	96	16.200	3.200	3. 4.	7. 6.15	H
LZ 39	39	24.900	161.4	2.800	"	85	11.000	3.000	24. 4.	18.12.15	H
L 10	40	31.900	163,5	4.300	4 x 210	96	16.200	3.200	13. 5.	3. 9.15	M
L 11	41	"	"	"	"	"	"	"	7. 6.	25. 4.17	M
LZ 72	42	"	"	4.000	"	"	"	"	15. 6.	16. 2.17	H
L 12	43	"	"	4.300	"	"	"	"	21. 6.	10. 8.15	M
LZ 74	44	"	"	"	"	"	"	"	8. 7.	8.10.15	H

1	2	3 cbm	4 m	5 km	6 PS	7 km/h	8 kg	9 m	10 vom	11 bis	12
L 13	LZ 45	31.900	163,5	4.300	4 x 210	96	16.200	3.200	23. 7.15	25. 4.17	M
14	46	”	”	”	”	”	”	”	9. 8.	23. 6.19	M
LZ 77	47	”	”	”	”	”	”	”	24. 8.	21. 2.16	H
L 15	48	”	”	”	”	”	”	”	9. 9.	1. 4.16	M
LZ 79	49	”	”	”	4 x 240	”	”	”	2. 8.	30. 1.16	H
L 16	50	”	”	”	”	”	”	”	23. 9.	19.10.17	M
LZ 81	51	”	”	”	”	”	”	”	7.10.		H
	U	35.800	”	4.900	”	95	17.900	3.500		27. 9.16	
L 18	52	31.900	”	4.300	”	96	16.200	3.200	3.11.	17.11.15	M
17	53	”	”	”	”	”	”	”	20.10.	28.12.16	M
19	54	”	”	”	”	”	”	”	27.11.	1. 2.16	M
LZ 85	55	”	”	”	”	”	”	”	12. 9.		H
	U	35.800	178,5	4.900	“	95	17.900	3.500			
LZ 86	56	31.900	163,5	4.300	”	96	16.200	3.200	10.10.		H
	U	35.800	178,5	4.900	”	95	17.900	3.500		4. 9.16	
LZ 87	57	31.900	163,5	4.300	”	96	16.200	3.200	6.12.		H
	U	35.800	178,5	4.900	”	95	17.900	3.500		28. 7.17	
LZ 88	58	31.900	163,5	4.300	”	96	16,200	3.200	14.11.		H
L 25	U	35.800	178,5	4.900	”	95	17.900	3.500		15. 9.17	M
L 20	59	”	”	”	”	”	”	”	21.12.	3. 5.16	M
LZ 90	60	31.900	163,5	4.300	”	96	16.200	3.200	1. 1.16		H
	U	35.800	178,5	4.900	”	95	17.900	3.500		7.11.16	
L 21	61	”	”	”	”	”	”	”	10. 1.	28.11.16	M
L 30	62	55.200	198,-	7.400	6 x 240	103	35.500	4.000	28. 5.	20	M
LZ 93	63	31.900	163,5	4.300	4 x 240	96	16.200	3.200	23. 2.	17	H
L 22	64	35.800	178,5	4.900	”	95	17.900	3.500	2. 3.	14. 5.17	M
LZ 95	65	”	”	”	”	”	”	”	31. 1.	22. 2.16	H
L 23	66	”	”	”	”	”	”	”	8. 4.	21. 8.17	M
LZ 97	67	”	”	”	”	”	”	”	4. 4.	5. 7.17	H
98	68	”	”	”	”	”	”	”	28. 4.	17	H
L 24	69	”	”	”	”	”	”	”	20. 5.	28.12.16	M
+)	70										
LZ 101	71	”	”	”	”	”	”	”	29. 6.	17	H
L 31-	72	55.200	198,-	7.400	6 x 240	103	35.500	4.000	12. 7.	1.10.17	M
LZ 103	73	35.800	178,5	4.900	4 x 240	95	17.900	3.500	8. 8.	17	H
L 32	74	55.200	196,5	7.400	6 x 240	103	35.500	4.000	4. 8.	23. 9.16	M
37	75	”	”	”	”	”	”	”	9.11.	20	M
33	76	”	”	”	”	”	”	”	30. 8.	24. 9.16	M
LZ 107	77	35.800	178,5	4.900	4 x 240	95	17.900	3.500	16.10.	17	H

THE GERMAN ARMY AND NAVY AIRSHIPS 1906-1918, WITH TECHNICAL DATA

1		2	3 cbm	4 m	5 km	6 PS	7 km/h	8 kg	9 m	10 vom	11 bis	12
L	34	LZ 78	55.200	196,5	7.400	6 x 240	103	35.500	4.000	22. 9.	27.11.16	M
	41	79	,,	,,	,,	,,	,,	,,	,,	15. 1.17	23. 6.19	M
	35	80	,,	,,	,,	,,	,,	,,	,,	20.10.16	18	M
LZ	111	81	35.800	178,5	4.900	4 x 240	95	17.900	3.500	20.12.	17	H
L	36	82	55.200	196,5	7.400	6 x 240	103	35.500	4.000	1.11.	7. 2.17	M
LZ	113	83	,,	,,	,,	,,	,,	,,	,,	22: 2.17	8.10.20	H
L	38	84	,,	,,	,,	,,	,,	,,	,,	22.11.16	29.12.16	M
	45	85	,,	,,	,,	,,	,,	,,	,,	12. 4.17	20.10.17	M
	39	86	,,	,,	,,	,,	,,	,,	,,	11.12.16	17. 3.17	M
	47	87	,,	,,	,,	,,	,,	,,	,,	11. 5.17	5. 1.18	M
	40	88	,,	,,	,,	,,	,,	,,	,,	3. 1.	17. 6.17	M
	50	89	,,	,,	,,	,,	,,	,,	,,	9. 6.	20.10.17	M
LZ	120	90	,,	,,	,,	,,	,,	,,	,,	31. 1.	30.11.20	H
L	42	91	55.500	,,	10.400	5 x 240	100	36.400	5.500	22. 2.	23. 6.19	M
	43	92	,,	,,	,,	,,	,,	,,	,,	6. 3.	14. 6.17	M
	44	93	55.800	,,	11.500	,,	104	37.800	,,	1. 4.	20.10.17	M
	46	94	,,	,,	,,	,,	,,	,,	,,	24. 4.	5. 1.18	M
	48	95	,,	,,	12.200	,,	107	39.000	,,	22. 5.	17. 6.17	M
	49	96	,,	,,	,,	,,	,,	,,	,,	13. 6.	20.10.17	M
	51	97	,,	,,	,,	,,	,,	,,	,,	6. 7.	5. 1.18	M
	52	98	,,	,,	,,	,,	,,	,,	,,	14. 7.	23. 6.19	M
	54	99	,,	,,	,,	,,	,,	,,	,,	13. 8.	19. 7.18	M
	53	100	56.000	,,	13.500	,,	109	40.000	6.500	8. 8.	11. 8.18	M
	55	101	,,	,,	,,	,,	,,	,,	,,	1. 9.	20.10.17	M
	57	102	,,	,,	,,	,,	,,	,,	,,	26. 9.		M
		U	68.500	226,5	16.000	,,	103	52.100	8.200		7.10.17	
	56	103	56.000	196,5	13.500	,,	109	40.000	6.500	24. 9.	23. 6.19	M
	59	104	,,	,,	,,	,,	,,	,,	,,	10.10.		M
		U	68.500	226,5	16.000	,,	103	52.100	8.200		7. 4.18	
	58	105	56.000	196,5	13.500	,,	109	40.000	6.500	29.10.	5. 1.18	M
	61	106	,,	,,	,,	5 x 290	,,	,,	,,	12.12.	28. 8.20	M
	62	107	,,	,,	,,	,,	,,	,,	,,	19. 1.18	10. 5.18	M
	60	108	,,	,,	,,	,,	,,	,,	,,	18.12.17	19. 7.18	M
	64	109	,,	,,	,,	,,	,,	,,	,,	13. 3.18	21. 7.20	M
	63	110	,,	,,	,,	,,	,,	,,	,,	4. 3.	23. 6.19	M
	65	111	,,	,,	,,	,,	,,	,,	,,	17. 4.	23. 6.19	M
	70	112	62.200	211,5	12.000	7 x 290	131	44.500	7.000	1. 7.	5. 8.18	M
	71	113	,,	,,	,,	7 x 260	,,	,,	,,	29. 7.	30. 6.20	M
	72	114	,,	,,	,,	,,	,,	,,	,,	9. 7.20	22.12.23	M